I0036459

The
Little
Black
Book
for Entrepreneurs

By Matthew Black

© **Copyright 2015 by Matthew Black**

Matthew Black has asserted his right under the copyright, designs and patents act 1988, to be identified as author of this work.

All rights reserved. No part of this publication may be reproduced, stored in a retrieval system, or transmitted, in any form or by any means, electronic, mechanical, photocopying, recording or otherwise, without the prior permission of the publisher or the Copyright Licensing Agency.

FIRST EDITION - October 2015

British Library Cataloguing in Publication Data

A catalogue record and a copy of this book are available from the British Library

ISBN: 978-1-910372-04-3

Parvus Magna Press publishes limited run and niche interest books in the UK. If you would like to see your book in print, please email your manuscript to *sharif@pmpress.uk*

Dear Reader,

I created this book to be written in, to be carried around, to capture hot leads, opportunities & inspired ideas.

As I approach my 30th year in business I look back, and autopsy my past business adventures. I have come to better understand the confluence of circumstances, resources, and thinking, which enabled my success in business.

The things I have learned, the tools I use, were all forged in the fires of failure, continuous refinement, and real world application in hundreds of businesses.

In this, my "Little Black Book" I will share some of the things that made me successful. I hope they work for you too.

Matthew Black

About the Author

Currently living in a salubrious part of London, Matthew was actually born and raised in a small dusty town in the wild untamed Australian outback. That's where he learned from local aborigines not just the skills, but developed the mental toughness, of being self-reliant, fearless, and driven to succeed; all essential to survive one of the most inhospitable landscapes in the world.

But equally valuable in the world of business. He is fond of telling stories from his outback adventures that have shaped his unique perspective and style of business. Combined with his larger-than-life character and business acumen it has earned him the title "The Outback Entrepreneur".

Matthew left home at 14, started his first company (logistics) at 18, selling it at just

20. Then founded Telecoms Company, valued at $55m before the age of 30.

His passion is Visioneering; helping founders clearly define their vision & direction. They then use the insights gained to reduce marketing costs, increase sales conversion by "engineering" the messaging and strategy.

Matthew has a personal goal of helping 1,000,000 people get started on the road to owning their own successful business by 2020. His books, various websites, videos and courses are all focused on achieving this outcome.

He is available to do public speaking and regularly works with future CEO's on his live streamed or online courses as well as bespoke 1:1 mentoring.

For more, information visit:

www.outbackguru.com
uk.linkedin.com/in/matthewvblack/

More great tips and advice go to

www.littleblackbook.tips

HEAD - more tips and insights into mindset for success:
http://outbackentrepreneur.com/more-from-the-little-black-book-head/

HEART – Advice on enjoying business, ethics and winning with style.
http://outbackentrepreneur.com/more-from-the-little-black-book-heart/

S&S – A sausage story, business model & marketing analogy, what's not to love?
http://outbackentrepreneur.com/241-2/

TOOLS & TIPS
Top 3 things you must do
Marketing yourself
My Pitch, tactics & lead capture

Printable resources at
www.littleblackbook.tips

Contents

HEAD

HEART

SIZZLE & SAUSAGE

TOOLS & TIPS

Organise Your Mind and the Rest Will Follow

HEAD

"In the kingdom of the blind,   the one-eyed man is king."

Desiderius Erasmus

What's Going on in There?

I have always had an interest in how my own mind works. I suppose it's because most of my early focus was sales-orientated, and the ideal salesman has a deep understanding of people. Thinking ahead of your prospect, high levels of empathy, understanding motivations as well as what social & physical cues to look for in terms of the buying process.

The most useful skills I think I have acquired in all my years in business have always been in the area of understanding people, drivers, limiters, motivators and distractors.

Knowing what & how your ideal prospect thinks is the single biggest advantage that any business can have.

The "Impossible" 4 Minute Mile

According to legend, experts once said the human body was <u>simply not capable of a 4-minute mile</u>.

In fact, the record of 4:01 stood unrivalled for over nine years and, despite numerous attempts, it took until 1954 for Roger Bannister to break "the barrier" with 3:59.4. Was he just faster?

No, in fact our research suggests he was ranked well below many others who had recently made an attempt to beat the record.

So what was his Winning Secret?

As part of his training, Bannister <u>relentlessly visualized the achievement.</u> He trained his mind in order to create a sense of possibility, as much as he trained his body for the task he was undertaking.

Today it's common, almost routine, and even high school children have broken the 4-minute mile barrier.

Nelson Mandela's powerful quote; "it always seems impossible until its done" hints at, an essential truth about humanity.

That our greatest limitation is frequently ourselves.

Less is more

Simplicity and clarity in all things lead to good brand, better customer engagement and much more. People just "get it".

Google is a perfect example of a 'solution focus'.

While other platforms added more and more things (news, weather, sports, video) into their homepages.

Google focused on one thing, the best search results, presented simply. After that they had a very smart plan to monetise, but it started with and continues to this day; the aim to solve the customers burning issue:

I just want to find stuff

"Big Fish in a Small Pond"

Companies that have over 40% of the market share in a niche typically get up to 250% better ROI for marketing than those who have under 10%.

NICHE ≠ SMALL

Niche can reduce your marketing expenses because you're more focused. Niche marketing is a way for a new business to enter a market. It allows you to concentrate your time and resources narrowly to maximize your effectiveness in gaining a foothold.

Niche too much or too long can leave you vulnerable to strong competition. Diversify once you have a strong business with organic growth in your Niche.

Find Big Problems not Big Ideas

One of the biggest mistakes a start-up can make is building a business on an idea.

Apps are particularly guilty of the 'idea trap'; that's why +90% never make any money. Simply they start with, "let's build a better, faster, more featured app than anyone else". It's flawed thinking, it's an arms race you can never win.

Ideas are great, but only if they come from "my idea fixes this <u>specific</u> problem". In fact, your perfect customer is one that has the biggest "pain" that you fix.

Ask yourself:

'Whose hair is on fire to get a hold of my solution?'

I CAN.
I WILL
End of story.

With all the hype out there you might be fooled into thinking that to achieve success you just have to have a "go for it" attitude. While this is critical, so is a sane decision making process & building your business in the real world.

DEMAND:
Do people want it?

EXECUTION:
Can I deliver on a plan & will I make money?

It sounds so simple, but trust me I meet people regularly that don't meet even this basic criteria. If you do NOTHING else, seriously, honestly answer these questions before you invest too much of your (or anyone else's) time and money.

My Top Tips for the Right CEO Mind Set

<u>Indecision is worse than failure</u>: at least if you fail you tried, and you might learn something. You're the boss; make a decision, live with the consequences.

<u>Stop asking permission</u>: poll staff, mentors, professionals for their opinion, that's just smart, but it's your business; if you're not going to drive it, who is?

<u>KNOW that you don't know everything</u>: You cannot do it alone; nobody has ALL the skills needed to succeed. Outsourcing to specialists makes financial sense.

<u>Business is a TEAM SPORT</u>: get people involved, share your vision, let them build the dream with you (allow contribution).

But remember it's your vision, <u>you need to be the biggest fan</u>.

A big part of a CEO's job is to motivate people to reach certain goals; inspire trust in investors, attract partners, affiliates and more.

Leadership can take many forms and is essential at many points. However, don't be alarmed; I will share with you the easiest and most powerful feature of being a good leader.

Firstly, be yourself, there is nothing as inauthentic as someone pretending to "Fake it Till you Make it". Secondly, leverage your clarity of vision- tap into your passion. Why are you doing this business? Why this product? Why this model?

Telling your story with clarity and passion will win hearts and minds. When you pitch or write marketing collateral pretend you're talking to an old friend. Try to share your true feelings. Trust me, if you tell people a story, heartfelt and honest, you will win not only supporters, but advocates.

<u>WARNING</u>

Validate your idea early or risk wasting time & resources on lost causes.

Failure to continually assess your assumptions will increase chances of business failure.

EARLY IDEA VALIDATION

The following pages are for capturing your idea as inspiration strikes you. My advice is to fill out as much as you can, as soon as you can.

Ideas are sometimes like light bulbs. They might appear in an instant, burning bright, illuminating all the possibility around you, but I have found they can blink out of existence just as quickly.

Please use the "My Genius Ideas" sheets for quick idea capture and some cursory internal testing before you go and speak to real people.

A4 Printable forms available at
www.littleblackbook.tips

MY GENIUS IDEA 1

"Perfect Customer"

_____

_____

Their problem

_____

_____

What will people pay to have this go
away?

£_____(LTV)

Your solution

_____

_____

_____

What's the business model?

_____

Is the market size sufficient and growing?

_____

Validation Score: **G**_____% **F**_____%

Notes

_____

_____

_____

MY GENIUS IDEA 1

"Perfect Customer"

_____

_____

Their problem

_____

_____

What will people pay to have this go
away?

£_____(LTV)

Your solution

_____

_____

_____

What's the business model?

_____

Is the market size sufficient and growing?

_____

Validation Score: **G**_____%   **F**_____%

Notes

_____

_____

_____

MY GENIUS IDEA 2

"Perfect Customer"

_____

_____

Their problem

_____

_____

What will people pay to have this go
away?

£_____(LTV)

Your solution

_____

_____

_____

What's the business model?

_____

Is the market size sufficient and growing?

_____

Validation Score: **G**_____% **F**_____%

Notes

_____

_____

_____

MY GENIUS IDEA 3

"Perfect Customer"

_____

_____

Their problem

_____

_____

What will people pay to have this go away?

£_____(LTV)

Your solution

_____

_____

_____

What's the business model?

_____

Is the market size sufficient and growing?

_____

Validation Score: **G**_____%   **F**_____%

Notes

_____

_____

_____

MY GENIUS IDEA 4

"Perfect Customer"

_____

_____

Their problem

_____

_____

What will people pay to have this go
away?

£_____(LTV)

Your solution

_____

_____

_____

What's the business model?

_____

Is the market size sufficient and growing?

_____

Validation Score: **G**_____%   **F**_____%

Notes

_____

_____

_____

MY GENIUS IDEA 5

"Perfect Customer"

_____

_____

Their problem

_____

_____

What will people pay to have this go
away?

£_____(LTV)

Your solution

_____

_____

_____

What's the business model?

_____

Is the market size sufficient and growing?

_____

Validation Score: **G**_____% **F**_____%

Notes

_____

_____

_____

MY GENIUS IDEA 6

"Perfect Customer"

_____

_____

Their problem

_____

_____

What will people pay to have this go
away?

£_____(LTV)

Your solution

_____

_____

_____

What's the business model?

_____

Is the market size sufficient and growing?

_____

Validation Score: **G**_____% **F**_____%

Notes

_____

_____

_____

31

For loads of ideas, or help bringing your
idea to life checkout www.lightbulb.city

REAL WORLD TESTING

If your idea passed the early internal assessment stages and seems on the surface to be viable, then the litmus test is, of course, the real world. Don't use excuses like "I need to build it first..." you need to be able to explain it; the features, the functionality and most importantly the benefits. If you can't get a potential paying customers involved then good luck getting investors to believe you. So start testing, as soon as you can, in the real world.

Customer survey *the Super-fast version*

Ask as many of your target market as possible.

Question: I believe you have (describe problem) and would pay for (solution)?

TRUE? How much? = potential gross rev per customer or

33

FALSE? feedback?

Validate everything

If you like the idea of a rating system to help you decide on which idea is the best one, here's a possible way to do just that.

Criteria 1 - Hot or NOT

Does the idea have "gravity", that special quality that means people just "get it" and more than that, they want it?

How "good" is the potential idea? $G = C \times A / 100$

C = Customer – are they willing/able, or already spending/losing money on a solution to their problem?*

A = Attractive – how attractive is the solution in reference how awful the problem you're fixing, AND how much competition do you have?*

Criteria 2 - Reality or fantasy

It is real? Can you create, market, sell and generate the revenue to make a profit? AND how much cash will you burn through to get it to break even? AND is it worth it? E.g. a £1M investment to create a business with an annual net profit of £500K = not worth it. Investors typically want **10x** return in **3-5 years**.

How "feasible" is the potential idea? **F = P x T /100**

P = Power – can you get the team, the skillsets you need, & attract the initial money needed to make this a reality?*

T = Technical - Is your idea achievable, have you got a prototype or accurately scoped the development & production costs?*

*all these questions should be rated 1-10 with 10 being the highest

HEART

"Our prime purpose in this life   is to help others.

And if you can't help them, at least don't hurt them."

Dalai Lama

What's your purpose?

What is your reason for going into business? Purely to be the boss? To make a lot of money?

I know from experience that you can start a business for all the right reasons, but sometimes those reasons get lost in the day-to-day grind, the fire-fighting and multitasking. Write here your reasons from embarking on this journey, if you feel lost, stressed in the future, I hope you find it again.

The reason I am starting a business is….

_____

_____

_____

_____

_____

_____

If I start a business will it fail?

Statistically speaking, <u>YES</u>.

It takes something special to be successful in business. We know this because the statistics tell us so:

About half of all start-ups fail within five years.

While these figures are alarming, factor in the number of good ideas that never see the light of day or start-ups that never incorporate, the likelihood of success is tiny. In fact it's probably the most risky thing you will ever do.

<u>But there is POWER in knowing that many will fail.</u> Hopefully you will not begin when under prepared, under resourced or under skilled.

The best strategy that I know to increase your chances of success is work with people whom have a track record of success.

Oh, and a backup plan, just in case.

"If you don't try at anything, you can't fail... it takes back bone to lead the life you want"

Richard   Yates

People say that risk is an essential component of business. I think that's true, but not really a factor for Entrepreneurs. For them, I think it's more emotional; it's fulfilling a vision.

It's with their vision in mind that they take the leap, usually from employment to starting a company for the first time. It is not usually logical, well thought out, calculated, planned risk, but worthy risk.

At the heart of their decision, the entrepreneur weighs out their motivations for success, their desire to reach a goal, their love of their Idea & its Impact, against the tangible and intangible risks of failure. Then they make a judgment call.

It is infinitely more of an emotional decision than a logical one, and that is why HEART is such a critical component in the success of any venture.

Heart can get you into a mess, but it can also get you out.

The logic of
validation allows us
to move between the
two limits of
dogmatism and
scepticism.

Paul Ricoeur

Top tips for avoiding pitfalls in business

I am self-taught and I see it as an advantage, because I never assume I know anything. I constantly test, *"Is this the right thing to do?"*

I make a deliberate effort to surround myself with specialists in a variety of fields. It gives me near instant access to test assumptions or decisions I make, before I am overcommitted to a course of action.

It's steered me clear of many a potential disaster. But it's not second-guessing, just constant searching for validation that the path I am is the right one.

I don't always need it, but when I get additional validation the confidence boost helps me go harder and with more power and velocity than I would if I had any lingering doubts in my mind.

Leap

out of bed

The Secret to Success Starts Here

Visualise exactly, being crystal clear, what "success" looks like for you with as much clarity and detail as you can. Then write it all down. In fact, this is usually how I start writing a business proposition or business plan.

This clarity of vision also serves well as the basis for sales and marketing content.

Create for yourself, your business or your life a vision with such power that it DRAGS you kicking and screaming towards success.

Make this vision big enough to scare you a little, yet inspiring enough that it gets you leaping out of bed in the morning excited for what's ahead.

Unleash
your inner
Entrepreneur

Do you believe?

Trust me; it's critical. A crystal-clear vision, backed up by a founder's complete faith, will get you there in the end.

<u>Write your overarching company vision here:</u>

_____

_____

_____

_____

_____

_____

_____

_____

_____

_____

_____

_____

Tip: try to make it "tweetable"; 140 characters or less in size. This constraint forces you to refine it to a high degree.

Credit to Forbes Contributor Carmine Gallo – I love his message map video

Your GFP

The Entrepreneur inside us all

Psychologists theorise that something called the General Factor of Personality (GFP) trait lies deep within our mind and influences what we usually perceive as our personality (the id). GFP is thought to be a primitive structure and measurement of "GFP potential" has been coined "evolutionary fitness". In short, a higher score means being better equipped to deal with the challenges life throws at you.

Starting and hopefully succeeding is often touted as the greatest, most challenging experience any person can undertake.

Obviously, this is a generalisation; I am sure Arctic explorers, our Special Forces etc. would have a lot to say about this statement, but for most I would say this is generally true. It's for this reason I would point to this "fitness" as being an almost perfect benchmark of your inner Entrepreneur.

Measuring
Your GFP

Attributes of a high GFP might be high degrees of mastery in these areas:

Self-Control - delayed gratification, goal setting

Calmness - think "James Bond"; cool, calm and collected.

Intellectual Curiosity - self-improvement, always seeing or thinking up opportunities, and "out of the box" thinking.

Positivity - social, engaging. People like happy people

Empathy - essential for leadership & marketing

"He who fails to plan, is planning to fail"

Winston Churchill

Get S.M.A.R.T.

SMART is an acronym used to remind us that goals should be Specific, Measurable, Attainable, Relevant and Time-bound.

"Goals", I hear you cry, 'that's for squishy life-coach types whom ask me to 'tell them your dreams....'" Call it your corporate strategy if you like, it's essentially the same thing. Goal setting is unequivocally proven to be a top tool for the success of any project.

You need to set goals around every key area of your business; first revenue, MVP, break even, bridging the "gap" and more.

Good goal setting should focus your efforts, help you manage resources and time, as well as beat out procrastination and time wasting activities.

Get smart and get some goals, people!

Sizzle

Let me tell you a story:

In Australia, at almost any big hardware store, you will find a little stand. It's usually run for, or by, a charity. They inevitably have a BBQ with a big bucket of ice cold drinks. PERFECT for someone in a DIY frame of mind on a baking hot Aussie Sunday afternoon.

Now, nobody goes there with a sausage in a bun on their mind, they are concerned about the leaky tap or their garden lawn dying. But they BUY sausages.

People smell the cooking onions, hear the sizzle of the sausages on the fire, smell the smoke and charred meat (a real caveman experience).

Basically as long as they can afford one, they **<u>WANT ONE</u>**.

That's sizzle…..

You and your Monkey brain

Sex, aggression, compulsiveness, worship, fear, greed.

These all have one thing in common, they are all basically emotional responses; controlled in part, sometimes completely, by the more primitive parts of our brain, deep in our heads. Sometimes referred to as the 'Monkey Brain' or the 'Reptilian Brain'. My preference is Monkey; it seems to gel with the "I WANT IT NOW" emotive buying that advertisers have been tapping into for over a century.

While most people are completely at the mercy of their "inner child", the entrepreneur can harness this power, for sales, to boost their productivity, drive through the tough times and more.

The trick is that I know, I might lead by my emotions, but I can choose to give in, or not, <u>and so can you!</u>

"If you can't explain it simply, you don't understand it well enough."

Albert Einstein

Unique selling points (USP's)

1.
_____

_____

_____

_____

2.
_____

_____

_____

_____

3.
_____

_____

_____

_____

Underpin each core point with 2-3 sub points. These must be specific, ideally factual. For example: statistics, quotes, things that support and enhance the core points your trying to make.

Credit to Forbes Contributor Carmine Gallo – I love his message map video

Unique selling points (USP's)

1.

2.

3.

Underpin each core point with 2-3 sub points. These must be specific, ideally factual. For example: statistics, quotes, things that support and enhance the core points your trying to make.

Credit to Forbes Contributor Carmine Gallo – I love his message map video

SAUSAGE

So... back to the story:

So we have the attention of our customer in potentia and their interest has been stimulated.

Their inner caveman is battering the logical brain **"BUY IT"**.

So, we have a sale. Or do we?

Not quite yet; you need sausages.

Obviously sizzle is only half the equation- you need to deliver on the promises it makes. For me Sausage is product, support systems, delivery and accounting systems.

Basically everything involved from the point of buying through to a satisfied customer and a completed transaction.

Why the long drawn out analogy? I see it again and again: both 'sizzle but no sausage' and 'sausage but no sizzle'.

You must have a balance.

Tools
&
Tips

The right (or wrong) tools can make or break a business

There are literally hundreds of options; apps, systems and process you can, should or must implement in your business.

Though it's way beyond the scope of this book to go into it, I will guide you to what you need to look for.

When you're starting out the core areas you need to concentrate on first are Customers & Operations. Basically your focus should be getting & keeping customers, while monitoring your business & protecting your interests.

"Get closer than ever to your customers.

So close that you tell them what they need well before they realize it themselves."

Steve Jobs

Customer Related

Get a CRM: No, Excel, Outlook and Gmail contacts are NOT CRM. There are plenty of free ones out there; the key is linking contact details with tracking what you're doing, have done, and plan to do so you can cultivate a **relationship** with that contact.

Get connected: Social media presence depending on your business needs, a web presence (even if it's just a one-page online brochure) and some kind of calendar (Google is fine, you can even publish availability if you want, invite & auto manage acceptance)

Say YES to opportunity: Getting your phone talking to your tablet, laptop or desktop isn't just cool, but in todays "always on" world you need to be able to get the clients files, book appointments or connect to colleagues anywhere, anytime.

> *"There are two levers to set a man in motion, fear and self-interest."*

Napoleon Bonaparte

Operations Related

Get legal: contracts, insurance, financial records, diarise renewals, regulatory obligations etc. My advice is find a good professional early; you will need them.

Keep track: Sales, cash and minimising costs are dear to the heart of all CEO's. Integrated systems called ERP are complex and expensive, but there are plenty of DIY integrations- even using free software. But cash and calendars are not your only thing to track as you grow it all gets "more". From hashtags to keywords, company passwords to where to all the email accounts point to- stay ahead of the curve by planning early.

People power: Essential to get the skills you need consider; co-founders working for "sweat equity", interns, apprentices, freelancers, maybe even volunteers.

Today's to do list

1.Start day

2.SMASH IT

3.Relax

Beating procrastination is a major hurdle for some people. You can use this stupidly simple, but incredibly effective tactic to stop running in circles and GET STUFF DONE.

Write down your personal to do list. These are the **TOP 3 THINGS YOU MUST DO TODAY** things that will drive your business forward.

1.

_____
_____
_____
_____

2.

_____
_____
_____
_____

3.

_____
_____
_____
_____

DO NOT help anyone else, answer emails or calls, and don't do <u>anything</u> else unless you finish that list.

Got a Pitch?

Elevator pitch

From Wikipedia, the free encyclopaedia

"An elevator pitch, elevator speech or elevator statement is a short summary used to quickly and simply define a profession, product, service, organization, or event and its value proposition."

A good 'elevator pitch' is almost essential in business.

You can grow your company vision easily into a pitch by adding up to three core points; unique selling points (USP's) that make your company stand out over the competition or that you really want your customers to know about you.

"Quality questions create a quality life.

Successful people ask better questions, and as a result, they get better answers."

Anthony   Robbins

The Perfect Pitch

You should always use your own words and deliver it in your own style, but this is a good general guide to get you started.

The only glaring thing missing is a call to action (CTA) that you should use at the end of a pitch.

An example of a CTA might be:

"If you know anyone I will give you £200 for every referral that turns into a paying client, who wants £200 for sending me an email? Anyone? Great, grab a card off me after this."

A CTA can vary so dramatically depending on the situation, you, your audience, even the stage they are at in their sales cycle.

Many people also like to add a qualification. For example, "I am looking for people who want a free 20 minute consultancy on how to grow their idea into a profitable business". This is great if you're keen to qualify if the listener is the right type of candidate.

My Pitch

Hi, Matthew Black, nice to meet you. If you haven't already guessed I am an Aussie, and I am a unicorn. (smile / lol)

Let me explain, firstly Australia has tiny population, 98% of which live in the big cities. But I was born and raised in a dusty outback town in the far north west of Australia, the real Aussie Bushman.

But though that makes me rare, what makes me really special, that Unicorn kind of special, is that:

I have been a Business Consultant, on three continents, for some of the largest companies in the world. Managed to become a millionaire, twice.

And almost everything I know about making money, about building a successful business, about winning at the game of life, I give away for free.

Would you like to know more?

Pitch Template

If you don't have a pitch use this form to help kick-start your thinking. But please remember to make it your own. If it's delivered comfortably and naturally in your own words, the chances of both people listening to the content, and developing trust, are infinitely higher.

My name is _____

and I am a _____

Typically, my clients are _____

_____

who have the challenge (their problem/pain)

_____

What they get from me is (takes away pain)

_____

For instance, (example of it working)

_____

Call To Action

_____

_____

"It's as important to sell yourselves as much as the service.

The business model's going to change 50 times, and the market's going to change, but you need to convince that investor that you are smart enough and excited enough about the opportunity that you'll figure it out."

Dylan Smith

Investor Pitch

An investor is interested in different things, so the pitch is different. Though this is rudimentary, and you will need to give a LOT more information to close a deal, this may just be enough to bag an appointment.

Hook (e.g. "unicorn") to grab attention.

_____

_____

_____

My company _____ is (creating solution) _____

Because <u>(insert customer)</u> feel (pain)

_____

_____

_____

We found (research = no/bad solution)

_____

_____

_____

How we (key differentiator/USPs)

_____
_____
_____
_____

We are (stage & progress so far)

_____

We are looking for (ask advice, money,
etc)

_____
_____
_____

GET
SOME

Sales, leads, opportunities, partners, advice, investment… Whatever you need, it's out there.

Go get it.

When attending events be

DELIBERATE.

I know it seems obvious, but I am constantly surprised by the number of people (more often staff of companies rather than Founder/CEO's) that fall naturally into social mode when attending events.

Don't chat, build rapport- and yes there is a difference.

Chatting is social and can continue all night with no objective.

Rapport looks the same, but ends as soon as you think you can ask them for something or to do something for you (like pay you some money).

Don't collect cards
Collect connections

If you want cold leads then use a phone book

Don't waste time at your precious networking opportunities grabbing up flyers or business cards, trust me, it's a waste of your time.

If you are meeting people face-to-face use that opportunity to discover more about them; who they are, what they want for themselves, if they like you & your business/idea.

The key to networking success is QUALITY of connections.

Note this stuff down in your LBB and use the insights you gained to create a potential client, investor, referee etc.

People do Business with that people they like

People ultimately choose to do business with people they like and everyone likes someone who shows interest in them. To quickly build rapport with someone you just need to remember **them,** and follow through.

Reflect back to them in your communications your common interests. Remember what they look like (so you can remember them next time). Remember under what circumstances you met, what you talked about, what their personality is like, what they do, what kind of business lead might they be interested in receiving etc.

It'll cost you very little and I guarantee that by remembering them, they will be sure to remember you. Use the following worksheet to make notes on events you attend, 1-2-1 interactions and action to take.

You would be surprised how many people REALLY WANT to do some business with me, then never follow-up afterwards.

"Anytime you find someone more successful than you are, especially when you're both engaged in the same business - you know they're doing something that you aren't."

Malcolm X

As previously mentioned, I am always surprised about how good business people, even sales professionals, forget to be professional when it comes to networking and trade shows.

Attack every event for what it is- a marketing exercise that costs you time and money. Research the event to ascertain any particular good opportunities, either to speak/present or offer sales materials (collateral). Can you/should you put up a popup banner or other signage? Sometimes for a small fee, sponsorship or even a donation to their favourite cause, you can stand out above the crowd. Well worth it if potential clients are in attendance.

Go early to me the host(s) before the event starts. They know the crowd and can point out potentially targets, even offer personal introduction if they like and trust you.

"You must measure to manage & refine to be competitive & stay profitable.

Finding exactly what to measure is the trick."

Matthew Black

Data is GOLD   when it comes to defining ROI,   which events work and why.

Like all marketing, you are probably wasting opportunities, time and money if you're not measuring and testing your marketing consistently. It's easy online, we have systems like analytics, to tell us who, when, and what people want, like, buy.   So consider applying the same metrics, strategy, and even methods (e.g. A/B test you pitch) to offline marketing.

The following sheets have space for you to fill in some rudimentary metrics for your next events. Cut/print them out and keep them in your pocket at these events. Also feel free to add your own that are be more relevant to you.

Note: regarding engagement; I like to measure how many people want to get quotes, accept a free or reduced price offer, and how many set up a meeting ON THE DAY, as well as afterwards. This is a good   indicator   of   two   things: networking/sales effectiveness and the quality/relevancy   of   the   audience.

Event/venue _____

Date _____ Speaker _____

Marketing metrics (estimates)

Audience No. _____ age range _____

Reach for pitch _____% 1-2-1 _____%

Results sales _____ offers _____

Insights?_____

Notes:

_____

_____

_____

_____

_____

_____

_____

_____

_____

_____

1-2-1's

Name, best contact, next meeting date/time

Face to face

and/or actions you need to take, by when

_____

_____

_____

_____

_____

_____

_____

_____

_____

_____

_____

_____

_____

_____

1-2-1's

Name, best contact, next meeting date/time

Face to face

and/or actions you need to take, by when

_____

_____

_____

_____

_____

_____

_____

_____

_____

_____

_____

_____

_____

Event/venue _____

Date _____ Speaker _____

Marketing metrics (estimates)

Audience No. _____ age range _____

Reach for pitch _____% 1-2-1 _____%

Results sales _____ offers _____

Insights?_____

Notes:

_____

_____

_____

_____

_____

_____

_____

_____

_____

_____

_____

1-2-1's

Name, best contact, next meeting date/time

Face to face

and/or actions you need to take, by when

_____

_____

_____

_____

_____

_____

_____

_____

_____

_____

_____

_____

_____

1-2-1's

Name, best contact, next meeting date/time

Face to face

and/or actions you need to take, by when

_____

_____

_____

_____

_____

_____

_____

_____

_____

_____

_____

_____

_____

_____

Event/venue _____

Date _____ Speaker _____

Marketing metrics (estimates)

Audience No. _____ age range _____

Reach for pitch _____% 1-2-1 _____%

Results sales _____ offers _____

Insights?_____

Notes:

_____

_____

_____

_____

_____

_____

_____

_____

_____

_____

_____

1-2-1's

Name, best contact, next meeting date/time

Face to face

and/or actions you need to take, by when

_____

_____

_____

_____

_____

_____

_____

_____

_____

_____

_____

_____

_____

_____

1-2-1's

Name, best contact, next meeting date/time

Face to face

and/or actions you need to take, by when

_____

_____

_____

_____

_____

_____

_____

_____

_____

_____

_____

_____

_____

_____

Event/venue _____

Date _____ Speaker _____

Marketing metrics (estimates)

Audience No. _____ age range _____

Reach for pitch _____% 1-2-1 _____%

Results sales _____ offers _____

Insights?_____

Notes:

_____

_____

_____

_____

_____

_____

_____

_____

_____

_____

_____

1-2-1's

Name, best contact, next meeting date/time

Face to face

and/or actions you need to take, by when

_____

_____

_____

_____

_____

_____

_____

_____

_____

_____

_____

_____

_____

_____

1-2-1's

Name, best contact, next meeting date/time

Face to face

and/or actions you need to take, by when

_____

_____

_____

_____

_____

_____

_____

_____

_____

_____

_____

_____

_____

Event/venue _____

Date ____ Speaker _____

Marketing metrics (estimates)

Audience No. _____ age range _____

Reach for pitch _____% 1-2-1 _____%

Results sales _____ offers _____

Insights?_____

Notes:

_____

_____

_____

_____

_____

_____

_____

_____

_____

_____

_____

1-2-1's

Name, best contact, next meeting date/time

Face to face

and/or actions you need to take, by when

_____

_____

_____

_____

_____

_____

_____

_____

_____

_____

_____

_____

_____

_____

1-2-1's

Name, best contact, next meeting date/time

Face to face

and/or actions you need to take, by when

_____

_____

_____

_____

_____

_____

_____

_____

_____

_____

_____

_____

_____

Event/venue _____

Date _____ Speaker _____

Marketing metrics (estimates)

Audience No. _____ age range _____

Reach for pitch _____% 1-2-1 _____%

Results sales _____ offers _____

Insights?_____

Notes:

_____

_____

_____

_____

_____

_____

_____

_____

_____

_____

_____

1-2-1's

Name, best contact, next meeting date/time

Face to face

and/or actions you need to take, by when

_____

_____

_____

_____

_____

_____

_____

_____

_____

_____

_____

_____

_____

_____

1-2-1's

Name, best contact, next meeting date/time

Face to face

and/or actions you need to take, by when

_____

_____

_____

_____

_____

_____

_____

_____

_____

_____

_____

_____

_____

_____

Event/venue _____

Date _____ Speaker _____

Marketing metrics (estimates)

Audience No. _____ age range _____

Reach for pitch _____% 1-2-1 _____%

Results sales _____ offers _____

Insights?_____

Notes:

_____

_____

_____

_____

_____

_____

_____

_____

_____

_____

_____

1-2-1's

Name, best contact, next meeting date/time

Face to face

and/or actions you need to take, by when

_____

_____

_____

_____

_____

_____

_____

_____

_____

_____

_____

_____

_____

_____

_____

1-2-1's

Name, best contact, next meeting date/time

Face to face

and/or actions you need to take, by when

_____

_____

_____

_____

_____

_____

_____

_____

_____

_____

_____

_____

_____

_____

- -

Event/venue _____

Date _____ Speaker _____

Marketing metrics (estimates)

Audience No. _____ age range _____

Reach for pitch _____% 1-2-1 _____%

Results sales _____ offers _____

Insights?_____

Notes:

_____

_____

_____

_____

_____

_____

_____

_____

_____

_____

_____

\-

1-2-1's

Name, best contact, next meeting date/time

Face to face

and/or actions you need to take, by when

_____

_____

_____

_____

_____

_____

_____

_____

_____

_____

_____

_____

_____

1-2-1's

Name, best contact, next meeting date/time

Face to face

and/or actions you need to take, by when

_____

_____

_____

_____

_____

_____

_____

_____

_____

_____

_____

_____

_____

_____

_____

- -

Event/venue _____

Date _____ Speaker _____

Marketing metrics (estimates)

Audience No. _____ age range _____

Reach for pitch _____% 1-2-1 _____%

Results sales _____ offers _____

Insights? _____

Notes:

_____

_____

_____

_____

_____

_____

_____

_____

_____

_____

_____

_____

1-2-1's

Name, best contact, next meeting date/time

Face to face

and/or actions you need to take, by when

_____

_____

_____

_____

_____

_____

_____

_____

_____

_____

_____

_____

_____

_____

_____

1-2-1's

Name, best contact, next meeting date/time

Face to face

and/or actions you need to take, by when

_____

_____

_____

_____

_____

_____

_____

_____

_____

_____

_____

_____

_____

Event/venue _____

Date _____ Speaker _____

Marketing metrics (estimates)

Audience No. _____ age range _____

Reach for pitch _____% 1-2-1 _____%

Results sales _____ offers _____

Insights?_____

Notes:

_____

_____

_____

_____

_____

_____

_____

_____

_____

_____

_____

1-2-1's

Name, best contact, next meeting date/time

Face to face

and/or actions you need to take, by when

_____

_____

_____

_____

_____

_____

_____

_____

_____

_____

_____

_____

_____

1-2-1's

Name, best contact, next meeting date/time

Face to face

and/or actions you need to take, by when

_____

_____

_____

_____

_____

_____

_____

_____

_____

_____

_____

_____

_____

_____

_____

HOT
LIST

People you meet that might help you turn your idea in to cash and your dream of being in business into a profitable company.

RATING 10/10

How urgent is it I follow up, research or partner with this person or company?

Next meeting date and time

_____

_____

Actions I need to take immediately:

_____

_____

_____

_____

_____

_____

_____

_____

_____

_____

RATING 10/10

How urgent is it I follow up, research or partner with this person or company?

Next meeting date and time

_____

_____

Actions I need to take immediately:

_____

_____

_____

_____

_____

_____

_____

_____

_____

_____

_____

RATING 10/10

How urgent is it I follow up, research or partner with this person or company?

Next meeting date and time

_____

_____

Actions I need to take immediately:

_____

_____

_____

_____

_____

_____

_____

_____

_____

_____

_____

RATING 10/10

How urgent is it I follow up, research or partner with this person or company?

Next meeting date and time

_____

_____

Actions I need to take immediately:

_____

_____

_____

_____

_____

_____

_____

_____

_____

_____

_____

RATING 10/10

How urgent is it I follow up, research or partner with this person or company?

Next meeting date and time

_____

_____

Actions I need to take immediately:

_____

_____

_____

_____

_____

_____

_____

_____

_____

_____

_____

RATING 10/10

How urgent is it I follow up, research or partner with this person or company?

Next meeting date and time

_____

_____

Actions I need to take immediately:

_____

_____

_____

_____

_____

_____

_____

_____

_____

_____

_____

RATING 10/10

How urgent is it I follow up, research or partner with this person or company?

Next meeting date and time

_____

_____

Actions I need to take immediately:

_____

_____

_____

_____

_____

_____

_____

_____

_____

_____

_____

RATING 10/10

How urgent is it I follow up, research or partner with this person or company?

Next meeting date and time

_____

_____

Actions I need to take immediately:

_____

_____

_____

_____

_____

_____

_____

_____

_____

_____

_____

RATING 10/10

How urgent is it I follow up, research or partner with this person or company?

Next meeting date and time

_____

_____

Actions I need to take immediately:

_____

_____

_____

_____

_____

_____

_____

_____

_____

_____

_____

RATING 10/10

How urgent is it I follow up, research or partner with this person or company?

Next meeting date and time

_____

_____

Actions I need to take immediately:

_____

_____

_____

_____

_____

_____

_____

_____

_____

_____

RATING 10/10

How urgent is it I follow up, research or partner with this person or company?

Next meeting date and time

_____

_____

Actions I need to take immediately:

_____

_____

_____

_____

_____

_____

_____

_____

_____

_____

_____

RATING 10/10

How urgent is it I follow up, research or partner with this person or company?

Next meeting date and time

_____

_____

Actions I need to take immediately:

_____

_____

_____

_____

_____

_____

_____

_____

_____

_____

_____

RATING 10/10

How urgent is it I follow up, research or partner with this person or company?

Next meeting date and time

_____

_____

Actions I need to take immediately:

_____

_____

_____

_____

_____

_____

_____

_____

_____

_____

_____

RATING 10/10

How urgent is it I follow up, research or partner with this person or company?

Next meeting date and time

_____

_____

Actions I need to take immediately:

_____

_____

_____

_____

_____

_____

_____

_____

_____

_____

_____

HELP!

How well do you recognize when you need help?

I don't care how smart or driven you are at some point in your career you will need to call upon others for help.

In fact, I think that this is probably THE most common mistake founders make in starting a business- not seeking help.

Whether that's recognising its time to hire an accountant or someone to help you market your company, realising when you need help is vital for your success.

Don't spending time on things that you can ask others to do, this frees you up to focus on what you're really good at. It is not only necessary, but it makes you a smart business owner and hopefully a successful one.

Make your own luck

When I look back at my life I have always thought about what's possible. How can I do things easier, better, faster? Always open to, and in fact actively seeking out, opportunities, connecting people, maximising meagre resources for maximum effect.

Now of course, a lot of it is luck and circumstance, but it's equally true that without someone being ready, eager in fact, to embrace the challenges of self-employment, and a persistent and pervasive habit of looking for opportunity, those 'chances' life throws at all of us would have drifted past unrealised.

"If you want my advice on the path to success; start by surrounding yourself with successful people"

Jonathan Pfahl

We all need inspiration. We all need a hand on our shoulder to guide us from time to time. I have had a number of mentors in my life and strongly advise you to do the same.

Choose people that you aspire to be like. Ideally they have been down the path you are seeking to go, know the pitfalls and are happy to make your journey easier than their own might have been.

A request: please make some notes, in this book or a journal, email things to yourself or make some videos, however you can. Capture any highs, lows, insights, traps, joys and disappointments of your journey.

Why? I hope you are here one day, where I am, right now, sharing **your** wisdom. Hoping that it will make a difference, making the path smoother for the next traveller.

Many thanks and good luck

With thanks for their contributions:

John Bickell of Trepisphere Ltd &
Bickell Consultancy,

Ketan Makwana & Jonathan Pfahl of
Rockstar Mentoring

Sharif George of The Sales Engine

Readers Bonus

As a reward for probably one of the few to get to the very end...

Drop me an email to and you can get not only my personal thanks, but a one off HALF PRICE deal on any book, video or consultancy that we offer.

Email to endofLBB@getred.co.uk

1. What you liked

2. What you didn't

3. Any other feedback

Printed in Britain
by
Parvus Magna Press

www.ingramcontent.com/pod-product-compliance
Lightning Source LLC
Chambersburg PA
CBHW070732220326
41598CB00024BA/3402